pop zone

DRAMA QUEENS

By Paul Coco

SCHOLASTIC INC.

New York   Toronto   London   Auckland   Sydney
Mexico City   New Delhi   Hong Kong   Buenos Aires

PHOTO CREDITS: Cover: (Olsen) Richard Stonehouse/Camera Press/Retna, (Lohan) Grayson Alexander/Retna, (Duff) Paul Smith/Featureflash/Retna, (Dunst) Patrick Robert/Corbis Sygma, (Vega) Robert Mora/Getty Images, (Hathaway) Steve Granitz/WireImage.com; Page 4: Leo Sorel/Retna; Page 5: (top left) Smeal Jim/Ron Galella/Gamma, (top center) Jeff Vespa/WireImage.com, (top right) James Devaney/WireImage.com, (bottom) Armando Gallo/Retna; Page 6: Sheryl Nields/Icon International; Page 7: (top left) Chapman Baehler/Retna, (top center) Carlo Allegri/Getty Images, (top right) Scott Gries/Getty Images, (bottom) Reed Saxon/AP Wide World Photo; Page 8: Beatrice de Gea/*Los Angeles Times*/Abaca; Page 9: (top left) Lucy Nicholson/Stringer/Getty Images, (top center) Tsuni/Gamma, (top right) Jeff Fusco/Getty Images (bottom) Jason Messer/Retna; Page 10: Armando Gallo/Retna; Page 11: (top left) Evan Agostini/Getty Images, (top center) Carlo Allegri/Getty Images, (top right) Elizabeth Lippman/ContourPhotos.com, (bottom) David Surowiecki/Getty Images; Page 12: Coliena Rentmeester/Icon International; Page 13: (top left) Arnaldo Magnani/Getty Images, (top center) Steve Granitz/Retna, (top right) Marcus Brandt/AFP/Getty Images, (bottom) Anthony Harney/Getty Images; Page 14: Raul Vega/Corbis Outline; Page 15: (top left) Raul Vega/Corbis Outline, (top center) Albert L. Ortega/WireImage.com, (top left) Dimitrios Kambouris/WireImage.com, (bottom) Tsuni/Gamma; Page 16: Sara De Boer/Retna; Page 17: (top left) Jeff Slocomb/Retna, (top center) Luis Martinez/AFF/Retna; (top right) Sara De Boer/Retna, (bottom) Steve Granitz/WireImage.com; Page 18: Chris Pizzello/ContourPhotos.com; Page 19: (top left) Catherine Steenkeste/NBAE/Getty Images, (top center) Alan Levenson/Time Life Pictures/Getty Images, (top right) Chris Pizzello/AP Wide World Photo, (bottom) Ron Galella/WireImage.com; Page 20: Armando Gallo/Retna; Page 21: (top left) Sheryl Nields/Icon International, (top center) Sheryl Nields/Icon International, (top right) Ernie Stewart/Retna, (bottom) Armando Gallo/Retna; Page 22: Rene Macura/AP Wide World Photo; Page 23: (top left) Gregg DeGuire/WireImage.com, (top center) Darla Khazei/Retna, (top right) Frank Micelotta/Image Direct/Getty Images, (bottom) Walter McBride/Retna; Page 24: Huckle/Morrison/AllActionDigital/Retna; Page 25: (top left) Lester Cohen/WireImage.com, (top center) Max Nash/AP Wide World Photo, (top right) Chris Pizzello/AP Wide World Photo, (bottom) Dave Hogan/Getty Images; Page 26: (top) Avik Gilboa/WireImage.com, (center) Vera Anderson/ContourPhotos.com; Page 27: (top) Armando Gallo/Retna, (center) Ric Francis/AP Wide World Photo; Page 28: (top) Henny Garfunkel/Retna, (center) Henny Garfunkel/Retna; Page 29: (top) Henny Garfunkel/Retna, (center) Sara De Boer/Retna; Page 30: (top) Linda Vanoff/Gem Entertainment, (center) Linda Vanoff/Gem Entertainment; Page 31: (top) Ashley Knotek/Snappers/WireImage.com, (center) Ashley Knotek/Snappers/WireImage.com

---

Designed by Rocco Melillo • Cover design by Louise Bova

Photo Editor: Sarah Maria Vischer-Masino

ISBN 0-439-66976-6

Copyright © 2004 Scholastic Inc.

**Published by Scholastic Inc. All rights reserved.
SCHOLASTIC and associated logos are trademarks and/or registered trademarks of Scholastic Inc.**

12 11 10 9 8 7 6 5 4 3 2 1   4 5 6 7 8 9/10

**Printed in the U.S.A.
First printing, September 2004**

Introduction

2004 is shaping up to be the year of the leading ladies on the silver screen. With so many young, talented women working in movies today, you might wonder where all the guys went.

Leading the way are superstars like Hilary Duff, Lindsay Lohan, and Katie Holmes. And there are plenty of newcomers like Brie Larson and Hannah Spearritt. This group of Screen Queens is here to stay!

And you'll find them all in this book. These young women are gifted actors – they love what they do, and they make movies you love, too! Keep reading to find out more about these big-screen stars. You just might be surprised to find out how much you share with your fave Drama Queen.

Katie Holmes

Can-do Katie

Best known as Joey Potter, Capeside's good girl on *Dawson's Creek*, Katie Holmes has spent the past few years establishing herself as a film actress. She's taken on serious roles and won rave reviews in films like *Pieces of April* and *Wonder Boys*. This year, she's out to cement her status as a bona fide movie star, playing Samantha Mackenzie in *First Daughter*. Samantha is the daughter of the President of the United States, who moves away to college to gain her independence. But, there's one catch: She falls in love with another student who's actually a Secret Service agent that has been assigned to protect her. Talk about your complicated relationships!

Katie calls *First Daughter*, "A mix between a mainstream and an art film," and compares it to an old black-and-white romance movie. "It's a coming-of-age story. Samantha is trying to become independent outside of her family, and that's not easy when you're the first daughter. She falls in love and there's a betrayal, but I think it's really sweet and funny."

Katie might not be the daughter of the President, but she certainly knows what it's like to live life in the public eye. She's already been on every magazine cover imaginable and she's bound to get more attention for her upcoming wedding to longtime boyfriend, actor Chris Klein. Katie says that even though she's

focusing on the future, she still thinks about her *Dawson's Creek* costars all the time. "I miss having breakfast with them in the makeup trailer," she says. "I went to Kerr Smith's wedding. It's weird, like when your siblings get married. It's like, ohhh! Wow! We're all growing up!"

No matter how big of a star she becomes, Katie will always stay grounded and work hard. "I know that careers can go up and down," she says. "I'd do television again. I'd produce. I want to do movies. I want to do theater . . . I'll dance on a street corner if I have to. I just want to be involved."

Stats:

BIRTHDATE: December 18, 1978
BIRTHPLACE: Toledo, Ohio
CURRENT RESIDENCE: New York, New York
SIBLINGS: Katie has three older sisters and an older brother
ASTRO SIGN: Capricorn
HEIGHT: 5' 8"   **HAIR/EYES:** Brown/hazel
FIRST MOVIE SHE EVER SAW: *E.T.* at a drive-in

Faves:

MOVIES: *My Best Friend's Wedding*, *Pretty in Pink*, and *Sixteen Candles*
MUSICIANS: Sarah McLachlan, Jewel, and the Dave Matthews Band
ACTIVITIES: Dancing, running, watching movies, and listening to music
JUNK FOOD: Jelly Bellies, cookie dough, buttered popcorn, and onion rings
DRINKS: Sugar-free soy vanilla lattes and Diet Coke   **RECENTLY READ:** *The DaVinci Code* by Dan Brown
HER DREAM ROLE: "I'd like to do some lush, romantic period piece where I get to wear gorgeous costumes."

fill-in faves:

Katie loves to watch movies at home. Your favorite movie is _____ because _____

_____

In *First Daughter*, Katie plays the President's daughter. How do you think your life would be different if your father was the President of the United States? _____

Mandy Moore

Mad About Mandy

It's hard to believe that it was only five years ago when a young Mandy Moore with bright blonde hair was singing "Candy." Critics dismissed her as a Britney wannabe, but Mandy was determined to prove them wrong.

Thanks to a star turn in 2002's tearjerker, *A Walk to Remember*, Mandy has gone from being a pop star to walking down the red carpet. She followed that role with the movies *Try Seventeen* and *How To Deal* in 2003 while releasing her fifth CD, *Coverage*.

Mandy has already released more records and starred in more movies than people twice her age, but she takes it all in stride. Balancing acting and singing were always part of her plan. "I knew that if I was involved in [the entertainment] industry, I wanted to try a little bit of both," Mandy says.

Think you've seen all there is to Mandy? Hardly! She's just getting started! In 2004, Mandy's back on the big screen playing Anna Foster in *Chasing Liberty* and Hilary Faye in *Saved*. Mandy says that one of the coolest things about *Chasing Liberty* was getting to spend a summer in Europe while the movie was being filmed. "The great thing is that I feel like I got to see a lot of each of the cities because we were constantly moving around to different locations," she says. "When we were at the fish market in

Venice, Italy, we were like tourists looking at all of the different stuff. I feel like I got to have a bit of a vacation being in all of these exotic locales."

Sure, Mandy stars in some really awesome movies, but what type of flick interests her? "I love romance and comedy and falling in love," she says. "That combination gets me every time."

Stats:

FULL NAME: Amanda Leigh Moore

BIRTHDATE: April 10, 1984   **ASTRO SIGN:** Aries

BIRTHPLACE: Nashua, New Hampshire

HAIR/EYES: Brown   **HEIGHT:** 5' 10"

SIBLINGS: Two brothers, Scott and Kyle

PETS: Three cats named Milo, Zoë, and Chloe

WHAT'S NEXT: Mandy lends her voice to the animated feature *Racing Stripes*

Faves:

BOOK: *A Walk To Remember* by Nicholas Sparks

CITY: New York, New York   **JUNK FOOD:** Peanut butter cups

ACTORS: Julianne Moore, Reese Witherspoon, and Audrey Hepburn

MOVIES: *Election* and *Roman Holiday*   **MUSICIANS:** John Mayer, Jason Mraz, and Coldplay

ENTERTAINMENT IDOL: Bette Midler   **MAKEUP:** Lip gloss by Deluxe

fill-in faves:

Mandy loves to sing and act. If you could choose any two talents, what would they be?

_____   _____

Mandy spent a summer in Europe filming *Chasing Liberty*. Where would you like to travel? _____.

Hilary Duff

Never Enough Duff

Like Madonna and Jennifer Lopez before her, Hilary Duff seems set to conquer Hollywood. Smash songs, mega-hit movies, and a too-cool clothing line make Hilary a true teen queen.

After soaring to fame with the Disney Channel series *Lizzie McGuire* and *The Lizzie McGuire Movie*, Hilary has barely had a minute of free time. Last year, she filmed the blockbuster *Cheaper by the Dozen*, and during the day she recorded her megamillion-selling first album, *Metamorphosis*. At night, she somehow found the time to do 3.5 hours of school work a day! It's almost impossible to imagine how she manages it all, but it doesn't matter, because everything that Hilary does turns out to be a success. Audiences are already hooked on Hilary's latest movie, *A Cinderella Story*. In it, Hilary plays Sam Montgomery, who is – believe it or not – an unpopular teen. She also has to deal with a nasty stepmother and two mean stepsisters. So not cool.

In the movie Sam starts e-mailing the guy of her dreams (played by *One Tree Hill's* Chad Michael Murray) but freaks out when she learns that he's the most popular guy in her school. Will Sam be courageous enough to reveal who she is, or will she let her Prince Charming get away? You'll just have to see the movie to find out.

Hilary truly has star power. There's just about no place she can go without getting recognized. Malls have even had to be closed down when too many kids swarmed around

her. How does Hilary handle her autograph-seeking fans? "There are definitely times I wish I could go unnoticed," she says. "You never think about what losing your anonymity is going to be like. Even now, when I am doing a signing and a lot of people show up, I wonder who they're there to see."

You might think that Hilary leads the life of a superstar 24/7, but Hilary says that just isn't true. She would rather hang out with her friends then attend a celebrity-filled bash. But she probably couldn't go to the party anyway. Hilary's mom sets a curfew, and she's not allowed to break it. No ifs, ands, or buts about it!

Stats:

NAME: Hilary Ann Lisa Duff   **NICKNAMES:** Hil and Juicy
BIRTHDATE: September 28, 1987   **BIRTHPLACE:** Houston, Texas
HEIGHT: 5' 4"   **HAIR/EYES:** Blonde/hazel
SIBLING: An older sister, Haylie
PETS: Three dogs — a border collie named Remington, a mixed-breed terrier named Lil' Dog, and a pocket Pomeranian named Bentley.
WHAT'S NEXT: Two feature films, *Heart of Summer* and *The Perfect Man*, another solo CD, and her own line of goods called Stuff by Duff to be sold at Target.

Faves:

CAR: BMW X5   **BOOK:** *Catcher in the Rye* by J.D. Salinger
CHILDHOOD BOOK: *Where the Sidewalk Ends* by Shel Silverstein
ACTOR: Sandra Bullock   **ATHLETE:** British soccer player David Beckham
VACATION SPOTS: Cancun, Mexico, and Hawaii   **FASHION BRANDS:** Louis Vuitton and Juicy Couture
JUNK FOOD: Doughnuts   **MOVIE:** *Drop Dead Gorgeous*   **CLOTHING ITEM:** Shoes   **CAN'T LIVE WITHOUT:** Chewing gum

fill-in faves

Hilary loves *Catcher in the Rye.* Your favorite book is _____ because _____

_____.

In *A Cinderella Story*, Hilary's character has to overcome her shyness. Was there ever a time you spoke up and had

something good happen? _____.

Lindsay Lohan

Look Out for Lindsay

Many people first discovered seventeen-year-old Lindsay from her movie role as Annabell Coleman in the Disney remake of *Freaky Friday* with Jamie Lee Curtis. While *Friday* might have pushed Lindsay into the spotlight, the New York City native has been in front of the camera since she was eleven, when she modeled for Abercrombie Kids and Calvin Klein. These modeling gigs landed her roles on the soap opera *Another World*, and soon after she hit the big screen in the remake of *The Parent Trap.*

Now, she's turning heads in *Mean Girls* and *Confessions of a Teenage Drama Queen*, based on the novels of the same name. In *Confessions*, Lindsay plays Lola, a teen who is unhappy about her family's decision to move out of trendy New York City and into the New Jersey suburbs. Lola spends a lot of her free time dreaming about her favorite rock group, who is about to break up. She'll stop at nothing to make it to the band's final concert and meet the lead singer, Stu Wolff. Will Lola meet her favorite rock star? You'll have to see the movie to find out.

Is Lindsay a drama queen in real life, too? "My character is a little more out there than I am," she says. "She lives every day as if she was acting out a movie." Lindsay says she has more in common with her *Mean Girls* character. Her character, Cady, plays the new girl at school who winds up breaking up the cool clique. Like many of her Drama Queen peers,

Lindsay is looking to release her debut album. She says the album will have a "rock/hip-hop vibe, like Liz Phair meets Pink." You can hear Lindsay's first song, "Ultimate," on the soundtrack to *Freaky Friday*. Combining music with acting is part of Lindsay's future plans. "I'd like to win an Oscar and a Grammy someday," she says. "I'd go on a tour and live like a rock star!"

Lindsay is very happy with her life and career at the moment. Fame is fun, she says, but she's even happier hanging with her friends. "I like the fact that I have my friends I can go home to, hang out with and be a normal kid," she says. "You only live once . . . I think it's important to be yourself." That sounds more like the confessions of a down-to-earth diva.

Stats:

FULL NAME: Lindsay Morgan Lohan   **NICKNAME:** Linds
BIRTHDATE: July 2, 1986   **ASTRO SIGN:** Cancer
BIRTHPLACE: Cold Spring Harbor, New York
CURRENT RESIDENCE: Lindsay shares an apartment with actress Raven Symone in Los Angeles
HAIR/EYES: Auburn/green
SIBLINGS: Brother, Michael and two sisters, Dakota and Aliana
NEXT UP: The feature film *Dramarama*

Faves:

SPORTS: Basketball and soccer   **CAR:** BMW 330 convertible
ICE-CREAM FLAVORS: Chocolate and vanilla   **MUSICIAN:** Liz Phair
INSTRUMENT: Guitar   **ACTORS:** James Dean and Brad Pitt   **FOOD:** Chinese
CLOTHING BRAND: Christian Dior   **CHILDHOOD BOOK:** *The Little Prince* by Antoine de Saint-Exupéry

fill-in faves

In *Confessions of a Teenage Drama Queen*, Lindsay's character dreams about seeing her favorite band in concert. Which band would you like to see in concert? _____

In *Freaky Friday*, Annabella wakes up one morning as her mother. If you could switch places with any person, who would it be?

_____.

Mary-Kate and Ashley Olsen

Totally Talented Twins

Could there possibly be any two people under the age of eighteen more famous than Mary-Kate and Ashley Olsen? Not likely. The famous duo grew up on TV — literally! Before they even turned a year old, Mary-Kate and Ashley took turns playing the role of Michelle Tanner on early '90s sitcom *Full House*. But that was a long time ago, and this year, the Olsen twins have their eyes set on much bigger projects, like turning eighteen and moving to New York City to start their freshman years at New York University. The Olsen girls plan on spending every possible minute together as roommates in New York City. "I can't wait to go [to college]," says Mary-Kate. "It'll be our first place away from our parents. We plan on living together. Not that I'm happy about doing laundry." Ashley couldn't agree more. "Going away to school is a great way for us to be more independent." And that's not all, they also have a new movie coming out called *New York Minute*.

New York Minute follows Jane Ryan (Ashley) and her sister, Roxy (Mary-Kate) for one day through Manhattan. They're two very different siblings who must work together to accomplish their goals. Jane is trying to get accepted to an overseas college program while Roxy is trying to sneak backstage to meet her favorite pop-punk band.

Are the sisters that different in real life? Yeah, right! They spend practically every second together and have never gone more than two weeks without seeing each other.

"We've been going to the same school since eighth grade and everybody knows us," says Mary-Kate. Ashley agrees, "I couldn't live away from [Mary-Kate]."

The future is wide open for the talented Olsen twins. They've made CDs, movies, DVDs, a clothing line, and tons of other stuff, but this year they're going to face their biggest challenge yet: final exams. Knowing Mary-Kate and Ashley, they'll do just fine.

Stats:

FULL NAME: Mary-Kate Olsen
NICKNAME: MK
BIRTHDATE: June 13, 1986
ASTRO SIGN: Gemini
BIRTHPLACE: Sherman Oaks, California
HEIGHT: 5' 1"
HAIR/EYES: Strawberry blonde/blue-green
RIGHTY OR LEFTY: Lefty
NEXT UP: The twins are taking some time off from acting to take classes at NYU.

Stats:

FULL NAME: Ashley Fuller Olsen
BIRTHDATE: June 13, 1986
ASTRO SIGN: Gemini
SIBLINGS: Twin sister Mary-Kate, younger sister Elizabeth, older brother Trent
HEIGHT: 5' 2"
HAIR/EYES: Strawberry Blonde/Blue-green
RIGHTY OR LEFTY: Righty

Faves:

COLOR: Blue
CHILDHOOD BOOK: *The Jungle Book* by Rudyard Kipling
SCHOOL SUBJECT: Psychology
FLOWER: Rose **MUSICIANS:** Aerosmith
JUNK FOOD: Ice cream **TV SHOW:** Friends
ACTOR: Tom Cruise **HOLIDAY:** Christmas
PASTIME: Pilates **COLLECTS:** Teddy bears

Faves:

CHILDHOOD BOOK: *Oliver Twist* by Charles Dickens **COLLECTS:** Candles
JUNK FOOD: Apple pie **TV SHOW:** Friends **PASTIME:** Horseback riding
TV CHANNEL: The Food Network **MUSICIANS:** The Rolling Stones
SCHOOL SUBJECT: Culinary (cooking) courses **ACTOR:** Tom Hanks

fill-in faves

Mary-Kate and Ashley get mistaken for each other all the time. Sometimes, people think you look like

_____ because _____.

Ashley collects teddy bears. What do you like to collect? _____

Alexa Vega

The 411 on the Sleepover Stars

If there's one movie you won't want to miss in 2004, it's *Sleepover*. Starring a who's who of up-and-coming actresses, led by *Spy Kids'* Alexa Vega, *Sleepover* is set the summer before a group of girls enter their freshman year in high school. Alexa plays Julie, head of the not-so-popular clique. Julie happens to throw her sleepover party on the same night the popular girls have theirs.

The fun really begins when they enter into an all-night scavenger hunt against the "cool" cliques led by Brie Larson's character, Liz. Winner takes all — dibs on the best lunch table in the high school.

Alexa and Brie hope that audiences will fall in love with *Sleepover* the way teens in the '80s and '90s loved *Pretty in Pink* and *Clueless*. Alexa says that it was important that *Sleepover* sent a fun message. "I'm in high school right now. I've already experienced regular junior high, so there's a lot of reality in this film [for me]," she says. "This has great messages in it about what you have to go through to be cool or whatever. It's something that I think young girls will enjoy . . . I wanted something with a love story, and this had it in there."

They may play archenemies in the movie, but Alexa and Brie became good friends on the set. The two talented teens found out that they had a lot in common since they had both grown up working in the biz.

Best known as Carmen Cortez from the *Spy Kids* movies, Alexa landed her first role back when she was only five! Back then, she played Burt Reynolds' daughter on the sitcom *Evening Shade*. She's come a long way!

Stats:

NAME: Alexa Ellesse Vega **BIRTHDATE:** August 27, 1988

BIRTHPLACE: Miami, Florida **ASTRO SIGN:** Leo

HEIGHT: 5' 4" **HAIR/EYES:** Dirty blonde/brown

SIBLINGS: Three younger sisters and one older half sister, named Margaux

HERITAGE: Half Columbian and half Italian

NEXT UP: The feature film *State's Evidence*

Faves:

CHILDHOOD BOOK: *The BFG* by Roald Dahl **VACATION SPOT:** Hawaii

SPORT: Water polo and gymnastics **FOOD:** Japanese **AUTHOR:** J.K. Rowling

ACTORS: Natalie Portman, Anthony Hopkins, and Jodie Foster

DRINK: Sunkist orange soda **CELEB CRUSH:** Josh Hartnett **CLOTHING BRAND:** Lucky

fill-in faves

If you were throwing a sleepover, you would invite

1. _____ 2. _____ 3. _____

You would stay up all night doing

1. _____ 2. _____ 3. _____

Alexa loves to make pizza. If you could put any three toppings on a pizza, they would be

1. _____ 2. _____ 3. _____

Brie Larson

Brilliant Brie

Brie got her start on the small screen, playing the daughter of a famous funnyman. As Emily on the WB series *Raising Dad*, Brie spent a lot of time goofing around her TV dad, played by Bob Saget. "We were always laughing so hard," Brie says. "He's so funny."

Brie and Alexa Vega bonded at a real sleepover that Alexa threw to get to know her costars better. "I think it really makes a difference when you know the people you're working with," Alexa says. "You feel more comfortable with everyone."

Alexa says she's getting used to starring in movies other than *Spy Kids*, but it was difficult when it came time to wrap up the series of movies that made her a star. "It was really sad," she says. "There was this giant good-bye and everyone on the set was bawling."

Now Alexa and Brie are looking forward to the challenges of meeting new people and working with different actors. "It's a little bit of a responsibility," Alexa says about taking on new projects. "You want to have a good time, but you really want to stay professional and focus on what you're doing." Alexa and Brie both agree that once the stress of filming is over, then the fun really begins.

Many teenagers would agree with Alexa's choice of fun activities: shopping, making pizza, and playing sports. Sounds like the stars of *Sleepover* are the type of people you'd want to invite to your own slumber party!

Stats:

FULL NAME: Brianne Sidonie Desaulniers
BRITHDATE: October 1, 1989
BIRTHPLACE: Sacramento, California
ASTRO SIGN: Scorpio
SIBLING: A younger sister named Milaine
PET: A Schipperkee dog named Roxy

Faves:

TV SHOW: Alias   **TYPE OF MUSIC:** Hip-hop
SPORTS: Basketball and cycling
PASTIME: Surfing, writing fiction, and dancing
CARTOON CHARACTER: SpongeBob Squarepants

fill-in faves

In *Sleepover*, Alexa and Brie fight over a lunch table in the high school. What's the silliest argument you ever got into with a friend? _____

_____ .

Sleepover is set during the summer before high school begins. Your favorite summer was _____

because_____

_____ .

Kirsten Dunst

Crazy Cool Kirsten

Kirsten Dunst became a star at age twelve, when she appeared with Brad Pitt in *Interview With a Vampire*, but after more than thirty films, it was a superhero that changed Kirsten into a superstar.

While many of her peers spent their teenage years making mindless horror flicks or cheesy date movies, Kirsten grew up on-screen starring in smash hits like *Bring It On* and in critically-acclaimed films like *The Cat's Meow* and *Crazy/Beautiful*.

As Mary Jane Watson, the love interest of Tobey Maguire's Spider-Man, Kirsten shot to the top of Hollywood's A-list and even got her own action figure. A real-life blonde, Kirsten says wearing the red wig helped her to portray Mary Jane as something more than just a damsel in distress. If blondes have more fun, then Mary Jane Watson proves that redheads have more attitude. "Mary Jane is definitely a hero," Kirsten says. "I got to do a fight scene in the rain. I was really happy to do it because I didn't want to look like the stupid girl who gets saved by the hero all the time. Mary Jane is a pretty strong woman . . . I felt sassy with the red wig on. Mary Jane is a very sassy girl."

With a career as red-hot as Mary Jane's hair, Kirsten's got two more starring roles in the coming year and a much-talked-about romance with heartthrob Jake Gyllenhaal. That doesn't mean that Kirsten likes to live a glamorous life. Kirsten's more likely to sleepover at her mom's house than be seen at the Hollywood hot spots. This girl is all about hanging out at home and relaxing. "I like tuna-fish sandwiches and pizza and bowling," she says. "I'm a big dork."

Don't expect any of that dorky behavior in this summer's *Spider-Man 2*. Kirsten won't reveal any secrets about the Spider-Man sequel except to say, "Mary Jane is a much stronger, more independent woman." Kirsten's already signed on to do a third *Spider-Man* film. *Spider-Man* had better watch out! If Kirsten has her way, the bad guys will be running from Mary Jane!

Stats:

NAME: Kirsten Caroline Dunst **NICKNAME:** Kiki

BIRTHDATE: April 30, 1982

BIRTHPLACE: Point Pleasant, New Jersey **ASTRO SIGN:** Taurus

CURRENT RESIDENCE: Los Angeles, California

EDUCATION: Notre Dame High School, Los Angeles, California

SIBLINGS: Younger brother, Christian

PETS: Four cats and a Yorkshire terrier, named Beauty

HEIGHT: 5' 7" **HAIR/EYES:** Blond/blue

NEXT UP: Two feature films, *Elizabethtown* and *Wimbledon*, a romantic comedy in which Kirsten will play a top-ranked tennis champ

Faves:

ACTORS: Jude Law, Gwyneth Paltrow, Jodie Foster, and Drew Barrymore

MUSICIANS: OutKast, Coldplay, Joni Mitchell, and Jeff Buckley **BOOKS:** *The Little Prince* and *The Great Gatsby*

SPORTS: Basketball (her favorite team is the Los Angeles Lakers) **ICE-CREAM FLAVOR:** Mint chip

SUMMER ACTIVITY: Staying at home with friends by the pool **MOVIE:** *Edward Scissorhands*

fill-in faves

Kirsten is learning to play tennis for her next movie, *Wimbledon*. One sport you would like to learn to play is

_____because _____.

If Kirsten came to my hometown, we'd spend the afternoon hanging out. We could do _____

_____together.

Sarah Michelle Gellar

Supreme Sarah

Jinkies! Those meddlin' kids — Sarah Michelle Gellar as Daphne, Freddie Prinze, Jr. as Fred, Matthew Lillard as Shaggy, Linda Cardelini as Velma, and their pal, Scooby-Doo — are at it again in *Scooby-Doo 2: Monsters Unleashed*.

In the sequel, the gang investigates the evil plans of an unknown villain who wants to take over the city of Coolsville by meddling with the "Monster Machine." The Machine makes copies of classic Scooby-Doo bad guys, such as the 10,000 Volt Ghost, Captain Cutler, and The Creeper. Fred and Daphne lead the team to the Coolsonian Museum where they discover some mysterious people and a whole lot of clues.

The first film was a huge hit, so it's no surprise that Sarah was all for doing a sequel. "When all these children came up to me and said, 'Scooby-Doo is my favorite movie,' that was great," says Sarah.

Growing up, *Scooby-Doo* was one of Sarah's favorite cartoons. "It was so far ahead of its time," Sarah says. "I thought that it was created in the '80s, when I was a child. [I did] not realize that it was created in 1969!"

Sarah's thrilled that she could be part of the team that brought the cartoon to life for a whole new generation of viewers. "I've learned to have a great love for comic books and cartoons and how much they mean to people," she says.

One thing she doesn't love: eating Scooby Snacks. They're not the same kind you can buy in the store. The ones used in the film didn't taste so hot. In fact, you might not even call them a snack. "They were this concoction that looked good on camera," Sarah said about the snacks. "By the fourth take, we were like, 'Someone get us a spit bucket, please.'" Gross! No more Scooby Snacks for Sarah, please!

Now that *Scooby-Doo 2* has been released, Sarah's getting to work in a movie that has something she's not used to: romance. As Buffy, Sarah slayed vampires and other demons all over Sunnydale, California, but she didn't really get much on-screen affection. In the upcoming spoof *Romantic Comedy*, Sarah plays Kate, a girl who remains clueless when her best friend, Max, tries to win her heart over by recreating things he saw in romantic movies.

Speaking of Buffy, is there any chance that Sarah would be interested in bringing the character to life on the big screen? "I'm not into it," Sarah says. "It didn't work as a movie. The reason the television show worked is because we did all these stories. I feel like we did one-hour movies every week." Hey, even a slayer needs some time off!

Stats:

NAME: Sarah Michelle Gellar

BIRTHPLACE: New York City, New York

CURRENT RESIDENCE: Los Angeles, California

BIRTHDATE: April 14, 1977   **ASTRO SIGN:** Aries

HEIGHT: 5' 3"   **HAIR/EYES:** Brown/green

PETS: Maltese Terrier named Thor and an Akita named Tyson

NEXT UP: The feature films *Romantic Comedy* and *The Grudge*

Faves:

SPORTS: Ice skating and football   **COLOR:** Red   **FOOD:** Pasta

COLLECTIONS: Antique books   **MOVIE:** *The Princess Bride*

VACATION SPOT: Bermuda

fill-in faves

Sarah couldn't stand the Scooby Snacks she had to eat while making the movie. What food do you totally hate?

_____:

If you could spend a day with Sarah, where would you take her to:

A. the mall.   B. your favorite restaurant.   C. to your school so you could hang out with all your friends.

Anne Hathaway

All About Anne

There aren't many actresses who land a role on a TV show, but then can't decide for sure if acting is meant for them. Yet, that's exactly the problem Anne Hathaway faced in 1999 when the drama series *Get Real* went off the air after just one season. Anne traded in movie scripts for textbooks and enrolled at Vassar College as an English major. But a funny thing happened to Anne after her first year of college: She became a Princess.

Not a real princess, of course—more like a royal klutzy geek. As Mia Thermopolis in *The Princess Diaries*, Anne played a young woman who learned she was royalty. The film was a huge hit, and Anne discovered that acting was definitely for her. "I had never been that happy," she says. "So, I might as well make a career out of it."

Now that career is on the fast track. Earlier this year, Anne starred in *Ella Enchanted*, a romantic fantasy with a modern-day twist on the Cinderella story. The story follows Ella, a young girl from a magical world in which she receives a birthday "gift" from a fairy named Lucinda. Ella is given the gift of obedience. That means she must do anything anyone tells her. Ella is stuck living with a greedy father and two nasty stepsisters. And the only thing that makes Ella's life a little happier is her true love, Prince Charmont.

What does Anne have to say about her prince? "He's the sort of guy who'll battle for your honor, kill ninjas, then turn around and recite poetry to you," she says. "But he can also be goofy and hop down the street with you laughing hysterically. He's perfect."

The prince, played by English actor Hugh Dancy, is not Anne's real-life boyfriend. In fact, the twenty-two-year-old says she's too busy for a relationship right now. After *Ella*, Anne's got two more movies coming out, including the sequel to *Princess Diaries*.

In *The Princess Diaries 2*, Mia is now settled in Genovia when she finds out about a new problem. As a princess, she is required to marry an Englishman she doesn't even know. The solution? Mia and her best friend, Lilly, hit the highway for a European road trip.

By the time 2004 is over, there's no doubt that Anne Hathaway is going to be royalty on-screen and off — Hollywood royalty, that is!

Stats:

NICKNAME: Annie

BIRTHDATE: November 12, 1982   **ASTRO SIGN:** Scorpio

BIRTHPLACE: Brooklyn, New York

CHILDHOOD HOME: Millburn, New Jersey

EDUCATION: Anne went to Vassar College to study English Literature

HEIGHT: 5' 8"   **NEXT UP:** The feature film *Havoc*

Faves:

PASTIME: Yoga   **ACTRESS:** Angelina Jolie

MOVIES: *All That Jazz* and *Pretty Woman*   **SPORTS:** Soccer and softball

BOOKS: *Beloved* by Toni Morrison and *Bluebird* by Kurt Vonnegut

SPORTS TEAM: New York Yankees   **MUSICIANS:** Tori Amos and Dido

COLLEGE SUBJECT: American politics   **PLACE TO SHOP:** The grocery store (Anne loves to cook)

fill-in faves

Anne loves to cook in her free time. What do you like to do in your free time? _____

_____.

In *The Princess Diaries 2*, Mia and Lilly take a road trip. If you could go anywhere with your best friend, where would you

go? _____.

Emma Watson

Emma Casts a Spell

It's pretty amazing to be Emma Watson. Not only does she get to work with a cute costar like Daniel Radcliffe, but she also gets to bring to life a main character from one of the most beloved book series of all times.

As Hogwarts School of Witchcraft and Wizardry's know-it-all, Hermione Granger has been turned into a cat, and petrified. It's certainly not easy work for a young actress, but fourteen-year-old Emma Watson says it's all part of the fun of playing the famous Harry Potter character.

How has Emma adjusted to seeing herself as a book character? "The first time you watch you're so freaked out about seeing yourself on-screen," she says. "The second time you kind of enjoy it. Then the third time you appreciate the film and the work that's gone into it, and you enjoy yourself."

Emma may not believe in having magical powers, but her bedazzling performance as a young witch-to-be has won her plenty of Muggle fans across the globe. Emma beat out thousands of young girls to play the part of Hermione, and was totally shocked herself when she landed the role. "I went to the audition for laughs," she says. "I never thought I'd get the part."

Despite the fact that she's known all over the world as Hermione, Emma has very little in common with her character. "I'm very different from Hermione," she says. "I'm not as obsessed with school as she is, but I still do quite well. I have a lot more time with my friends . . . we like to spend time talking and hanging out . . . I love to play sports. I am also much more obsessed with clothes and shopping, whereas Hermione has no fashion sense whatsoever."

Though she may be clueless when it comes to clothes, there are some things Hermione is good at, like getting rid of annoying boys. "There's a great scene [in the *Prisoner of Azkaban*] where I punch Draco Malfoy, which is really good fun," Emma says. "He runs away! Woo hoo! Girl power!"

There are some guys, however, that Emma says she'd be happy to have as her friends. When asked what she has enjoyed the most since becoming famous, Emma said, "I met Brad Pitt, which is quite cool."

Stats:

FULL NAME: Emma Charlotte Duerre Watson
NICKNAME: Em
BIRTHDATE: April 15, 1990   **ASTRO SIGN:** Aries
BIRTHPLACE: Oxfordshire, England
HEIGHT: 5' 6"   **HAIR:** Blonde
SIBLING: Younger brother, Alex
PETS: Two cats, Bubbles and Domino
NEXT UP: *Harry Potter and the Goblet of Fire*

Faves:

SPORT: Field Hockey   **FOOD:** Italian   **JUNK FOOD:** Chocolate
LIP GLOSS: Stila   **MOVIE:** Shrek   **ACTOR:** Brad Pitt
VACATION SPOT: The island of Mauritius in the Indian Ocean   **GADGET:** iPod
CLOTHING BRANDS: Diesel and Miss Sixty   **HARRY POTTER CHARACTERS:** Hagrid and Dobby

fill-in faves

Emma's character, Hermione, studies all the time. Your favorite class is _____because

_____.

Hermione learns all about magic powers. If you could have any magical power, it would be _____

because_____. 25

Jennifer Garner

Just Jennifer

Ballet dancing was Jennifer Garner's first love, but the acting bug bit her when she was an undergraduate at Ohio's Denison University. She had blink-and-you'll-miss-them roles in the WB series *Felicity* and the Ashton Kutcher movie, *Dude, Where's My Car*, but it was her role as butt-kicking CIA agent Sydney Bristow on the ABC series *Alias* that rocketed her to fame. "I've never felt more powerful as a woman," she says about the spy series. "I'm strong and more confident, and I know it's from playing Sydney." Now, Jennifer is branching out to a lead role in the comedy *13 Going on 30*, in which she plays a girl who wakes up one morning in the body of a businesswoman. And if she was feeling powerful before, just wait for her to take on some serious bad guys in the *Daredevil* spin-off, *Elektra*, in which she brings the role of the comic book character Elektra Natchios to life.

Stats:

FULL NAME: Jennifer Anne Garner
BIRTHDATE: April 17, 1972 **ASTRO SIGN:** Aries
CHILDHOOD HOME: Charleston, West Virginia
NEXT UP: The feature films *Happy Endings* and *Elektra*

Faves:

JEAN BRAND: Seven **SPORT:** Kickboxing
PERFUMES: Kate Spade, Vera Wang, and Marc Jacobs
SNACK: Toast with butter and honey
PASTIMES: Cooking, gardening, and hiking

fill-in faves

Jennifer loves to have toast with butter and honey when she winds down after a long day. When you want to relax, you like

to _____:

In *13 Going on 30*, Jennifer plays a teen who wakes up as an adult. What do you think your life will be like when you're 30?

_____:

Halle Berry

Halle's Happening

No stranger to bringing comic-book characters to life on the big screen (she has played Storm in two *X-Men* movies), Halle Berry returns to the screen this summer playing the title role in *Catwoman*. She plays Patience Prince, a graphic designer who works in a big city, until one day, she finds herself being able to see at night, run very fast, and jump really high.

Halle says there's no mistaking her Catwoman for Michelle Pfiffer's character in the early '90s hit *Batman Returns*. "I'm my own incarnation, not to be compared with the others," Halle says. "I was nervous about living up to the women who have played her before. If I couldn't bring anything different, then why do it?"

As Catwoman, the Academy Award-winner has to avoid being caught by a detective who is out to expose her secret. Halle studied a form of Brazilian martial arts called capoeira for the role. "It's definitely more edgy," says Berry. "Catwoman is all about empowerment." It looks like Storm may have met her match!

Stats:

FULL NAME: Halle Maria Berry **BIRTHPLACE:** Cleveland, Ohio
BIRTHDATE: August 14, 1966 **ASTRO SIGN:** Leo
NEXT UP: The feature films *Nappily Ever After*, *The Guide*, and *The Set-Up*

Faves:

ACTRESSES: Jodie Foster and Julia Roberts
ROLE MODELS: Oprah Winfrey and Maya Angelou
SINGER: Lena Horne **CLOTHING ITEMS:** Shoes
COLLECTS: African art and porcelain dolls

fill-in faves

Halle won an Oscar for one of her movie roles. Have you ever won an award for something you did? _____.

If so, what did you win and what did you win it for? _____

_____.

Halle loves shoes. If you could go shopping with Halle in any store, it would be _____

Julia Stiles

Stiles' Style

In 2000, Julia Stiles did something that most up-and-coming actresses would never think to do: go to college. Though Julia had gotten rave reviews for her work as Kat in *10 Things I Hate About You*, she decided that getting her college degree was more important than any movie role, so she entered New York's prestigious Columbia University as an English Literature major. It was a decision that couldn't have made her happier. "School is really stimulating," she says. "Being in college is the leap from being a teenager to being an adult. It has exposed me to so much literature and art that I would've never otherwise been exposed to."

Now that Julia has only one year left as an undergraduate, she's focusing on the future. In the past year, she's starred alongside Julia Roberts in *Mona Lisa Smile*, fell in love with a Danish prince in *The Prince & Me*, and now she's ready to take to the stage. "I've really, really, really wanted to get back onstage," she says. "I'm going to do a production of *Oleana* in the West End in London. That was a big goal for me. I really love it."

Stats:

FULL NAME: Julia O'Hara Stiles **BIRTHDATE:** March 28, 1981
BIRTHPLACE: New York, New York **HEIGHT:** 5' 7"
SIBLINGS: Younger brother and sister
WHAT'S NEXT: The feature films *Romance & Cigarettes* and *The Bourne Supremacy*

Faves:

BOOKS: *The Unbearable Lightness of Being*, *Stories from the Dustbowl*, and *East of Eden*
AUTHORS: Milan Kundera, David Sedaris, and John Steinbeck
SPORTS: Soccer **SPORT TEAM:** New York Mets
MUSICIANS: The White Stripes

fill-in faves

Julia attends Columbia University in New York City. I think it would be fun to go to _____

_____ for college. I might study _____.

Julia loves to listen to the White Stripes. What's your favorite band? _____.

Kristen Stewart

Can't Catch Kristen

Kristen Stewart may only be fourteen years old, but she's already worked with some major Hollywood talent. She got her big break as Sam Jennings in the independent flick *The Safety of Objects*, which also starred *Dawson's Creek*'s Joshua Jackson. Afterwards, Kristen landed the role of Sarah Altman, Jodie Foster's daughter, in the too-close-for-comfort thriller, *Panic Room*. Scoring the *Panic Room* role wasn't a piece of cake. Kristen had to try out six times before she got the part. Talk about hard work for someone who was just eleven years old at the time.

The future is looking bright for Kristen. Her film, *Speak*, debuted at the Sundance Film Festival, and she's earned tons of new fans playing Maddy Phillips in the junior spy adventure *Catch That Kid*. The movie follows three kids who go on a near-impossible mission to get money to pay for an operation for Maddy's father. "I think [*Catch That Kid*] shows that if you have a best friend, you help them no matter what happens," Kristen says. With the help of Gus, a gadget guru, and Austin, a computer hacker, Maddy puts her rock climbing skills to the test to help her father.

And if you think acting is a challenge, it's nothing compared to rock climbing. "Trust me, rock climbing is a lot harder than you think," Kristen says. "You have to have major strength."

Stats:

FULL NAME: Kristin Marie Stewart
BIRTHDATE: April 9, 1990   **ASTRO SIGN:** Aries
BIRTHPLACE: Colorado, USA   **HEIGHT:** 5' 3"
CURRENT RESIDENCE: Los Angeles, California
SIBLING: Older brother, Cameron

Faves:

SPORT: Surfing
FOOD: Sushi
MUSICIANS: Green Day, U2, and Nirvana
ACTOR: Jodie Foster

fill-in faves

In *Catch That Kid*, Maddy needs help from two friends. When did you need help from your friends to solve a problem? How

did they help? _____.

Kristen loves to surf. What's your favorite thing to do when you go to the beach?

_____.

AnnaSophia Robb

Amazing AnnaSophia

Haven't heard of AnnaSophia Robb yet? Well, that's about to change because this ten-year-old newcomer landed the lead role of India "Opal" Buloni in *Because of Winn-Dixie*. The movie is based on the popular book by Kate DiCamillo.

In the movie, AnnaSophia plays Opal, a girl who moves to a small town in Florida. She adopts a stray dog and names him after the local grocery store. Opal and Winn-Dixie explore their new town together and along the way, meet some very interesting people.

AnnaSophia, who is a total dog lover, loved working with the five dogs that played Winn-Dixie. "When I got the part I was really excited to hear there was going to be a dog working with us . . ." she says. "When we were in rehearsal, I just wanted to hug them and give them doggie biscuit treats."

AnnaSophia isn't the only newcomer in the flick. Music superstar Dave Matthews makes his first big-screen appearance as a pet shop owner. Some of AnnaSophia's favorite scenes were filmed in the pet shop. "The animals go crazy and we have to catch them," she says. "[The crew] let the pigeons go and one flew at my mouth. I was disgusted!"

Stats:

HOMETOWN: Denver, Colorado

BIRTHDATE: December 8, 1993

NICKNAME: "O.P." (She got the name while playing the character "Opal.")

Faves:

ANIMAL: Dogs

SCHOOL SUBJECTS: Music and computers

fill-in faves

AnnaSophia loves dogs. My favorite animal is _____ because _____

_____.

Anna names her dog after a grocery store. The craziest pet name I've ever heard is _____

Hannah Spearritt

Hip Hannah

You may have never seen Hannah on the big screen before, but chances are you have heard her music. For the past five years, Hannah was a member of the superpopular British group S Club. The group split in 2003, and now Hannah's pursuing her interest in acting. "Acting's my first love," she says. "I don't see myself really going back to the music side."

There certainly will be no going back for Hannah after audiences see her awesome work in this year's action flick, *Agent Cody Banks 2: Destination London.* In the new film, Hannah plays undercover agent Emily Summers. She and Frankie Muniz have to stop a madman who's trying to take over the world by controlling people's minds. Sounds like an easy job, huh?

In fact, the role of Emily wasn't so easy, especially for Hannah who hadn't worked with any of the cast before. "It was very intimidating," she says about coming into the sequel. "The fact that the first film did really well was a little bit of a pressure." Hannah says she just tried to make the best of a nervous situation. "You try to gain as much experience from working with these great people," she says. "You just try and get better." There's no doubt that things will only get bigger and better in Hannah's future!

Stats:

FULL NAME: Hannah Louise Spearritt
NICKNAME: Spanner **HEIGHT:** 5' 4"
BIRTHDATE: April 1, 1981
BIRTHPLACE: Great Yarmouth, England
SIBLINGS: An older brother and sister

Faves:

MOVIE: *Chicago* **VACATION SPOT:** Sydney, Australia
SCHOOL SUBJECT: Math
AMERICAN CITIES: New York, New York and Santa Monica, California
CHILDHOOD BOOK: *Charlotte's Web* by E.B. White

fill-in faves

Hannah was nervous filming *Agent Cody Banks 2* because she didn't know any of the cast and crew. The last time you were

nervous was _____

because_____.

 **Quiz** So just how much do you know about your favorite actress? Take this quiz to test your knowledge.

1. **KATIE HOLMES GOT HER BIG BREAK IN WHICH WB SERIES?**
   A. *Felicity*
   B. *Roswell*
   C. *Popular*
   D. *Dawson's Creek*

2. **MANDY MOORE GOT TO HANG OUT IN WHICH EUROPEAN CITY WHILE FILMING _CHASING LIBERTY_?**
   A. London, England
   B. Paris, France
   C. Barcelona, Spain
   D. Venice, Italy

3. **TEENS HAVE BEEN FANS OF THIS SINGER AND ACTRESS EVER SINCE SHE STARRED ON THE DISNEY CHANNEL SERIES *LIZZIE MCGUIRE*. SHE IS?**
   A. Raven Symone
   B. Melissa Joan Hart
   C. Hilary Duff

4. **THIS ACTRESS SAYS THAT SHE'S NO DRAMA QUEEN:**
   A. Lindsay Lohan
   B. Jennifer Garner
   C. Sarah Michelle Gellar

5. **MARY-KATE AND ASHLEY OLSEN CAN'T WAIT TO GO TO WHICH UNIVERSITY?**
   A. Columbia
   B. Harvard
   C. New York

6. **ALEXA VEGA IS BEST KNOWN FOR PLAYING WHICH SPY CHARACTER?**
   A. Sidney Bristow
   B. Carmen Cortez
   C. Emily Summers

7. **KIRSTEN DUNST STARRED WITH WHICH MOVIE HEARTTHROB IN *INTERVIEW WITH A VAMPIRE*?**
   A. Tom Green
   B. Brad Pitt
   C. Jesse Thomas

8. **YOU'RE LIKELY TO FIND WHICH ACTRESS HANGING OUT IN SUNNYDALE OR COOLSVILLE?**
   A. Sarah Michelle Gellar
   B. Halle Berry
   C. Linda Cardelini

9. **BAD GUYS DON'T STAND A CHANCE AGAINST JENNIFER GARNER IN THE HIT SPY SERIES:**
   A. *Alias*
   B. *Buffy the Vampire Slayer*
   C. *Teen Titans*

10. **WHICH ACTRESS STARRED AS CATWOMAN?**
    A. Julia Stiles
    B. Kirsten Dunst
    C. Halle Berry

ANSWERS: 1.D 2.D 3.C 4.A 5.C 6.B 7.B 8.A 9.A 10.C